The Affordable Care Act is *Working!*

A Special Report on Cost Savings

Election Edition

Since its passage in 2010, the ACA has annually:

- ➤ Saved employed families an average of $2,600
- ➤ Lowered Medicare costs by $1,000 per senior
- ➤ Saved Uncle Sam $100 billion

All while *INCREASING COVERAGE*—
   providing health insurance for 28 million more citizens!

All while *IMPROVING STANDARDS OF CARE*—
   resulting in 1.3 million fewer hospital-acquired Illnesses!

Robert L. McCan, Ph.D.

First 2016 Election Edition published June 2016.

ISBN-13: 978-1534679610

ISBN-10: 1534679618

Before **the Affordable Care Act:**

Between the years 2000 and 2010 health insurance premiums increased by 8.5% annually. Never once in 50 years did the increase fall below 5%.

--Kaiser Family Foundation

After **the Affordable Care Act:**

From 2010 to 2013 National Health Expenditures grew just 1.1%, the slowest rate of any three year period on record.

--President's Council of Economic Advisors, September 24, 2014

For Medicare the average growth per year has been 7.7% annually. During the first three years of the Affordable Care Act growth was between 2% and 3% annually. It increased in 2013 to 3.4%....

--The Henry J. Kaiser Family Foundation, July 2014

Preface

In the most dramatic and hard-fought political battle of our time—after decades of failed attempts by both Democratic and Republican presidents—Democrats in 2010 finally succeeded in passing the Patient Protection and Affordable Care Act (ACA).

Democrats demonstrated their commitment to making quality affordable health care available to every American through their years of thorough study and tough negotiations to get it through Congress. They were driven by the humane desire to eliminate the old "pay or die" system in which Americans in ever increasing numbers were priced out of the market. At the same time, they shared a practical commitment to shaping a law that would keep money in the national treasury and in the threadbare pockets of the American people.

Republicans constantly proclaim themselves as the "fiscally responsible" party trying to balance the national budget. They portray Democrats as the party of "tax and spend."

The very different approaches of the two parties to a national health care system reveal that nothing could be further from the truth. Democrats approach this task with an eye to expanding coverage and improving the quality of care *while lowering costs*. Republicans—committed to unfettered profit-taking within the "free market" capitalist system—oppose virtually every cost-saving measure in the Affordable Care Act.

Democrats' primary client is the American people. Republicans' primary client is the Medical-Industrial Complex. Their clear agenda is to get the best deal possible for providers of health care at the expense of the people.

Very few of us are aware of the many ways the Affordable Act is designed to save money. The law is complex and is hard to explain in sound bites. Frankly, Democrats have done a poor job of educating the public about the ACA. The citizenry does not have enough accurate information to counter Republican scare tactics.

Realizing how many aspects of the ACA are still not understood by the American public, I published a 170-page book in 2014, Citizen's Guide to Health Care Reform, 2nd Edition, The Affordable Care Act Explained and Updated. In June 2016 I published a more scholarly and much longer version of this book by the same title. Scholars who want careful footnotes and expanded understanding are directed to that book.

This book is a summary version that highlights the most important elements of the June 2016 book—especially the many cost saving aspects of the law that have received little or no press coverage and are virtually unknown among the public.

-- Bob McCan

Introduction

An Overview

We had three compelling reasons to pass the Affordable Care Act of 2010:

- **Provide every citizen with insured health care**
- **Improve the quality of care throughout the system**
- **Control run-away costs**

The crisis was deepening in each of these areas.

Millions were Losing Health Insurance

The cost of health insurance kept going up. In 2010 at least 30 million Americans had been priced out of the market. The working poor had no money left after basic living expenses to buy it. Millions had cancelled their policies each year as costs skyrocketed.

Tens of thousands more each year were declared ineligible because of preexisting conditions or because insurance companies set limits on how much they would pay a patient in a given year.

These 30 million American citizens never had access to a doctor, to a hospital, or to needed drugs unless they were in a life-threatening crisis. Then they could walk (or be carried) into any hospital and receive needed emergency treatment, no matter how expensive.

Quality of Care was Deteriorating

We were less aware of the crisis in the quality of health care. For example, most doctors, hospitals and pharmacies were still writing prescriptions and medical directives by hand rather than by computer. An estimated million mistakes a year were made because of lost pieces of paper, hard-to-read directives and inscrutable prescriptions.

While millions had no access to a doctor's office, those with insurance and money were often over treated with procedures and drugs they didn't need, doing more harm than good.

One in three persons who entered a hospital in the United States came away with an infection, a mishandled procedure or some other harmful result—all paid for by you and me, usually through our insurance. 100,000 persons died each year because of hospital errors and inconsistent implementation of hygiene and other best practices.

Health Care Costs were Escalating

Between the years 2000 and 2010 insurance premiums shot up 8.7% annually. Never once in 50 years did the annual increase drop below 5%.

Large corporations complained about their competitive disadvantage with other nations because our health care costs were twice as much as in any other country. Employers were cutting back on benefit packages and requiring employees to pay an ever greater amount. Smaller businesses were dropping coverage entirely.

The self-employed faced dramatically higher costs for insurance than those in large consumer pools.

There was talk of health care costs bankrupting the nation. Many thought Medicare would be the first to go.

The Nation Had Little Choice but to Act

Democrats in Congress, led by President Obama, crafted the Affordable Care Act based on the model constructed and supported by Republicans and implemented in Massachusetts by Mitt Romney, a Republican governor—because they felt they had little choice. The nation was in a crisis and had to be rescued from disaster. Democrats would accept the Republican plan—their second choice—in order to satisfy Republicans and get the nation's financial house in order.

The Affordable Care Act was the nation's response both to a health crisis and a financial crisis. Then something unbelievable happened. Republicans rejected their own plan, crafted for them by the conservative Heritage Foundation. They did not bother to hide their reason. If President Obama and Democrats proposed it, they would obstruct its passage in every way possible. If it passed, they would try to block its implementation in every way possible—even by spreading wildly false information and repeating it daily. Amid this torrent of slander, Democrats pressed forward, asking the American people to give the new law a chance to work.

The Affordable Care Act is working! The focus of this book is to understand the many little-known ways the new health care law is working to bring costs under control.

Chapter 1

Taming our Out-of-Control System

How We Got Our "Medical-Industrial Complex"

How did we go from service-oriented family doctors to the medical-industrial complex that was devouring our economy in 2010? How did health care evolve from a way to help others into a huge industry dedicated to profits?

Insurance companies grew in size and wealth and took control of the health care system, keeping for themselves 25% to 28% of every dollar of an insurance premium and making billions in profits annually.

The American Medical Association set the rates by which doctors were paid and kept raising them arbitrarily over the years. Specialists began to charge thousands of dollars a day for their services. Physicians added "profit centers" that over-prescribed for their own clients. Without oversight, the medical profession failed to self-screen incompetent doctors.

Hospitals set their own prices, usually inscrutable to the public. Corporations began to buy hospitals in affluent areas and rake in billions of profit from them.

Drug companies acquired the right to set prices that could not be challenged—then constantly raised prices for essential life-saving drugs.

We, the citizens, became victims of powerful players in a mindless system. We got priced out of the market. We were held hostage where we were most vulnerable—with our health—even with our lives!

Managing This Out-of-Control System

The Affordable Care Act is our first systematic attempt to control the greed, to replace inefficient systems that are costly, and to install incentives that save money.

Those who designed the ACA did not expect to prevent costs from growing—only to slow the rate of growth through prudent policies and oversight—*while simultaneously achieving universal coverage and improving quality of care and better health outcomes for all*. The new law does address the prices we pay our doctors, our hospitals, our drug companies, our medical device makers, and the profits we allow our health insurance companies. The philosophy behind the ACA is that medical providers and industries should be treated fairly, **but we demand that they also treat the people fairly**. Further, we are in the process of shifting our orientation from a "sickness system" to a "wellness system" by emphasizing ways to become and stay healthy rather than simply treating illness.

The cost-control aspects of the ACA have received very little media attention, and few Americans know about these successes of the ACA.

The ACA is creating a culture that values and expects cost control. We are no longer willing to tolerate flagrant profiteering in the health care field. We are rooting out fraud and abuse. We are creating new structures for health care delivery that greatly improve quality and outcomes while dramatically lowering costs.

This is good news for a nation weary of skyrocketing medical costs--while families struggle to make ends meet.

Chapter 2

A Report Card: It's Working!

In this chapter we consider macro—big picture--statistics that tell the story of overall costs and reveal that health care spending is coming under control. In subsequent chapters we unlock the mystery of *how these cost savings are being achieved*.

Health Costs by the Numbers

For perspective on how much we pay for health care as compared to the other nations of the world, we go to the Organization for Economic Cooperation and Development (OECD). In 2012 our nation spent an average of $8,745 for every citizen on health care, almost twice as much as any other country in the world. The average spent among the top 32 countries was $3,484. Yet when we compare health care quality and length of life, these other countries have outcomes superior to ours. For example, in 2012 life expectancy in the U.S. was 78.7 years, while the average of the 32 countries was 80.2.

The cost of health care has slowed dramatically since the ACA became law. A 2014 report stated, "From 2010 to 2013 National Health Expenditures grew just 1.1%, the slowest rate of any three year period on record and well below the average rate of 4.6% from 1960 to 2010."

The Congressional Budget Office announced on March 9, 2015, "The ACA will cost $142 billion less over the next 10 years, compared to what the agency had projected on January 11."

For Medicare the average growth per year from 1969 to 2012 was 7.7%. For the first three years of the ACA growth was between 2 and 3% annually. It increased in 2013 to 3.4%, bringing the total cost of Medicare to $585.7 billion. Medicare spending was virtually flat in 2014. In 2015 Medicare cost $1,000 less per senior than it would if the ACA had not been enacted into law.

The Kaiser Family Foundation did a study that measured the growth of premiums for employer-sponsored insurance plans for families. Kaiser found that the average family-based policy grew by 4.2% in 2015, up from 3% in 2014. The report concluded that--*had premium growth since 2010 maintained the rate it had been growing for the 10 years prior to the ACA--the average policy for a family would be $2,600 higher than it actually was* with *the ACA!*

The 2016 Report

What is happening to the Affordable Care Act in 2016? First, we hear Republican voices sounding alarm bells in a make-believe world of disaster. Ted Cruz claimed in a campaign speech on January 21, 2016 in New Hampshire that his personal insurance premium had gone up by 50%. He gave the impression that this ungodly spike in price was commonplace. A reporter who investigated found that Ted Cruz and family had a Blue Cross/Blue Shield policy in 2015 that was not offered in 2016. He had the choice of getting another policy with the same company or going to a different company. The new policy that he chose with another insurance company had an entirely different range of benefits, accounting for the different price. Premiums in Texas in 2016 are up 4% on average over 2015.

Donald Trump says at virtually every campaign rally, as if it were true, that he will "repeal and replace 'Obamacare' because the rate increases are out of control. They are going up 30%--40%--even 50% each year."

It is quite astounding to observe that the ACA is bringing costs under control while at the same time providing health insurance in 2016 for 15 million additional persons in the expanded Medicaid program and 13.1 million more who signed for insurance through the federal website, most of whom receive government subsidies in order to afford their insurance.

The bottom line is that the ACA has reduced the ranks of the uninsured from 19% of the total population to 10% now, while bringing the total cost under control.

2016 is the fifth straight year that total health expenditure has increased less than 5%. Not once in the 50 years before the ACA passed in 2010 had we EVER achieved a rate increase as low as 5%! Indeed, between the years 2000 and 2010 the average annual rate of increase was 8.7%.

The Centers for Medicare and Medicaid Services (CMS) did an analysis of the 2016 rate of growth for the "Silver Plan," the one 70% of those with subsidized insurance choose. By June 1, 2015, insurance companies had proposed rate increases that averaged 10% for 2016. By the time rates were actually set in November, the states had negotiated that average down to 7.5%--still a larger than average increase under the ACA. The President's Council of Economic Advisers analyzed this spike in prices and attributed it to the added cost of medical care for those now covered who did not previously have health insurance. The Council said, "It is not a surprise or a cause for concern to see a temporary period of faster growth as newly insured individuals [with more health problems] begin to access care."

Many employed persons see their health insurance costs go up and unfairly blame the ACA. The confusion is not surprising. Employers choose health insurance for their employees and then decree how much of the premium the employees must pay out of pocket. The share paid by the employee keeps going up—from 6% of the total premium five years ago to 33% today. The employees pay more-- not because the cost of insurance has gone up but because management wants to shift costs to workers. Yet, the ACA is blamed by opponents for the increased amount paid by employees.

Chapter 3

Paying for the ACA

Additional Costs of the ACA

Yes, the ACA costs a lot of money. We must pay for Medicaid expansion and we must subsidize insurance premiums for those who cannot afford the entire cost of insurance. The ACA provides funding for states to set up their healthcare exchanges, buy their computers, train their staffs, and investigate and possibly challenge insurance company rate hikes that seem unreasonable. Some $25 billion is given to physicians and hospitals to upgrade their computer systems in the service of better health and greater efficiency. Billions are set aside for research into alternative delivery systems, basic medicine, and public health campaigns. These and other items will cost over a trillion dollars within 10 years.

Those who wrote the law found ways to cover these costs and then generate an equal amount of additional savings. We will now consider the sources of new income that are offsetting the new costs of the ACA.

New Taxes and Fees

The Affordable Care Act builds in an array of taxes and fees that virtually pay the cost of administering the law. Most of the excise taxes were agreed to by the major providers of services because each believed it would obtain 20 to 30 million additional paying customers—and this new income would more than offset these new taxes.

Here are the major sources of income built into the law:

- Medicare tax on wealth (going to Hospital Trust Fund) $420 billion in 10 years

- The tax on "Cadillac" insurance plans $150 billion in 10 years

- Health insurance company excise tax $116 billion in 10 years

- Insurance company excess compensation tax $50 billion in 10 years

- Pharmaceutical companies' fee $35 billion in 10 years

- Medical device tax on sales $13 billion in 10 years

- Tanning salon retail tax of 10% $3 billion in 10 years

- Other lesser taxes and fees combined $153 billion in 10 years

These taxes and fees are projected to generate $940 billion dollars over 10 years to largely defray the cost of the Affordable Care Act. They were scheduled to go into effect across several years. However, lobbying arms of some corporations and associations have succeeded in postponing the starting dates of some fees.

Savings from Eliminating Fraud and Abuse in Medicare

Members of Congress had long known that Medicare was being defrauded of billions of dollars each year. The ACA raised the budget for the anti-fraud unit in Medicare and developed new programs that detect and crack down on fraudulent sales of medical equipment and supplies. Each year into the ACA greater progress is being reported in saving money through fraud prevention and recovery of funds. Over $25 billion has been reported saved over the past five years.

Fraud and Malfeasance among Physicians

The ACA is requiring greater transparency throughout the health care system with the goal of eliminating dishonest billing and inferior practices. The American Medical Association long opposed open books, arguing the right of privacy. Medicare now requires that every physician make all charges public. On April 9, 2014 Medicare released information nationwide for the first time on the billings of individual doctors who treat Medicare patients.

The new data revealed that Medicare paid doctors $64 billion in 2012. Medicare paid 4,000 physicians in excess of $1 million each. Medicare found that some doctors charged for services they did not perform. Others used more procedures than were in the best interests of their patients, and others prescribed more expensive drugs as a way to increase their income. (They were paid 6% of the cost of the drugs for overhead and administration rather than a flat fee, incentivizing them to prescribe the most expensive possible drugs.)

Major cases of fraud were uncovered. Three big cases serve as examples:

- Farid Fata, a cancer physician in the Detroit area made intentional misdiagnoses and ordered unnecessary treatments--including chemotherapy—for patients who did not have cancer. Medicare expects to recover $91 million.

- Asad Qamar in Ocala, Florida collected more than $18 million from Medicare in 2012. A lawsuit accuses Dr. Qamar of billing Medicare for unnecessary operations. Nearly every patient who came in with any problem underwent surgery

- Solomon Melgen of West Palm Beach, Florida received the most from Medicare of any physician in 2012, a total of $21 million. $11.2 million went to injecting an expensive drug into the eyes of patients. Medicare was charged $2,000 for each injection. However, a cheaper generic drug that gets equal results would have reduced the cost from $21 million to $800,000. Dr. Melgen was jailed in Palm Beach on April 15, 2015 for scamming Medicare out of $105 million over several years.

Cracking down on fraud and abuse is expected to save Medicare 3% of its total expenditure.

Chapter 4

Hidden Savings from Universal Coverage

Most people are not aware of how reducing the number of uninsured can save money. The authors of the ACA included amendments to explain these cost savings and justify the mandate that everyone should be covered.

Ways Uninsured Citizens Increase Systemic Costs

The Institute of Medicine of the National Academies performed longitudinal studies from 2002 to 2014, concluding that our national economy loses up to $207 billion a year because of the poor health of the uninsured.

Another popular study conducted at Harvard University and published In 2009 showed that at least 45,000 people die annually due to lack of health insurance. Dr. Andrew Wilper, the lead author, stated, "We doctors have many ways to prevent death from hypertension, diabetes and heart disease—but only if patients can get into our offices and afford their medications."

The diabetes epidemic is one important example of the high cost of lack of insurance. When diabetes is caught early and controlled, treatment costs are relatively low, and patients can maintain reasonably good quality of life and well-being. Untreated diabetes however—all too common among the uninsured—becomes life-threatening over time. Patients go blind and lose feet and legs. Their kidneys fail, requiring dialysis and kidney transplants. They need frequent very expensive emergency treatment to stay alive.

A recent study revealed that 22% of Medicaid persons with diabetes began getting treatment for the first time after their state began participating in the expanded Medicaid program. Think of the untold human suffering avoided and the massive savings realized in long-term treatment costs for this population!

Three Added Savings from Universal Coverage

1. Uncompensated Hospital Care

The American Hospital Association reported that it cost hospitals $45.9 billion in 2012 to treat patients without insurance who could not afford to pay. Hospitals are required by a 1985 law passed under Ronald Reagan to treat any medical emergency. Hospitals pass much of this charity cost along to the insurance companies, and they pass it along to families who have insurance in the form of increased premiums. The average family that purchases health insurance pays an added $1,000 each year to compensate hospitals for uninsured people who cannot pay their bills. This cost will be eliminated when we all have insurance.

2. The cost of bankruptcy

62% of all bankruptcies are caused by high medical expenses. Families are wiped out because they don't have insurance or because they don't have enough insurance. In 2013 alone, 1.7 million persons declared bankruptcy due to medical expenses. The financial and emotional cost of bankruptcy is enormous, while the medical community and the economy also take a hit. When these 1.7 million bankrupt persons have adequate insurance policies, most of this financial loss and stress on the social system will be avoided.

3. Humanitarian and Economic Costs of Hospital Closures

Hospitals in communities with a high incidence of poverty are hit hard when states opt out of Medicaid coverage. There are not enough patients with health insurance to offset those who cannot afford to pay. As a result hospitals are going bankrupt and closing their doors, depriving large swaths of poor communities of any hospital service and destroying what is often the major source of jobs and income for the community. The problem is solved when states are vested in the ACA. Medicaid expansion and subsidized insurance restores the fiscal health of the hospitals.

States invite major savings when they sign up for Medicaid expansion. A recent study of these savings in Kentucky and Arkansas, the two states that benefitted most from the law, found that their participation will yield a combined savings of more than $1 billion over seven years.

Chapter 5

Restructuring Health Care Delivery

"The Committee [of the Institute of Medicine] calculated that about 30% of health spending in 2009—roughly $750 billion—was wasted on unnecessary services, excessive administrative costs, fraud and other problems. Moreover, inefficiencies cause needless suffering. By one estimate, roughly 75,000 deaths might have been averted in 2005 if every state had delivered care at the quality level of the best performing state."

--The Institute of Medicine, Press Release

This highly prestigious Institute of Medicine says our health care system is expensive, wasteful and harmful. This annual $750 billion of waste provides both the challenge and the opportunity for the Affordable Care Act.

The Atlantic magazine published a much-discussed article based on the Institute of Medicine study. Brian Fung, the author, broke down the annually wasted $750 billion into six categories:

- 27.5% is unnecessary services

- 24.8% is excessive administration costs

- 17% is inefficient care delivery

- 13.7% is inflated prices

- 9.8% is fraud

- 7.2% is prevention failure

Accountable Care Organizations (ACOs)

The Affordable Care Act supports the reorganization of much of our health care delivery system into Accountable Care Organizations, as the most effective way to confront each of the above categories of waste and improve quality of care.

An ACO is an organized group of family physicians, medical specialists and support personnel closely associated with a hospital. To be recognized it must agree to provide a "medical home" to a minimum of 5,000 clients who live in the same geographical area, usually a cross-section of economic strata.

The "fee for service" model is replaced with a single payment amount [insurance premiums of everybody in the ACO?] that covers all medical costs for a year. Employees of the ACO work for annual salaries, with added incentives for good work that lowers cost and improves quality. All costs and treatments are transparent, and reports are available to clients and to the public on the internet. Savings from this efficient and effective approach to medical care are shared among the ACOs, the clients and the government.

Quality of care is monitored in five areas:

(1) Effective treatment of the medical problem,

(2) Patient's reaction to the experience,

(3) Extent and efficiency of coordination of care among the entire medical staff,

(4) Patient safety, as measured by incidence of medical errors, and

(5) Degree of emphasis on wellness and prevention.

How the ACOs Save Money

The money wasted each year in the old system of medicine can be broken down in another way:

- Single physician or small group practices are inherently inefficient, with higher cost of office space, staff, multiple forms, staff insurance, etc.
- Poor quality and careless medical practice are tolerated with little oversight or transparency,
- Lack of coordination and consultation between primary care physicians and specialists leads to ineffective treatment,
- Large-scale overuse of doctors, hospitals and treatments are commonplace for those with health insurance or money who have no incentive to save,
- The "fee for service" model encourages overuse and inefficiency.

The ACO concept is not new. It is based on highly successful models that have been developed in both the private and the public sectors

Community Health Centers—A Government-Supported Model

Community Health Centers (CHCs) were originally established in the 1960s as part of the "War on Poverty" to serve the poor and the uninsured, primarily in medically underserved areas. The Affordable Care Act infused $11 billion plus $2 billion from stimulus funds into the CHCs to upgrade and expand the system.

By 2014 there were 1,200 Centers operating at 9,000 service delivery sites. They provide medical homes for 21.1 million patients in every state and the District of Columbia. The Centers employ 10,000 physicians and 7,500 nurses. Over 1,100,000 homeless people are enrolled. This successful model of convenient, comprehensive community-based health care delivery with medical providers under salary contributed to the ACO concept.

Kaiser Permanente—A Private Non-Profit Pioneer

Kaiser Permanente was formed in the early 1970s under the visionary leadership of Henry Kaiser in California. The ACO now has nine million patients in nine states and the District of Columbia. Kaiser operates with 14% overhead and profit, as compared to traditional policies with insurance companies who are permitted by law to take 20% in overhead and profit. Kaiser consistently gets highest marks for outstanding quality of care and low cost of treatment.

Kaiser members choose among several physicians for their primary care at the Kaiser complex in their community. The physicians record everything by computer and provide the patient with a copy at the conclusion of the session. Laboratories for tests and specialists for second opinions or specialized treatments are all under the same roof, making it easy for the patients to get the care they need conveniently and for the doctors to coordinate the patients' care.

Medical records and lab results are quickly available and easily accessible to everyone involved in the patient's care.

The medical staff is of high quality, on salary, and glad to be out from under the burden of managing an office, reporting to insurance companies, paying malpractice insurance, and keeping up with latest findings in medicine without a community of colleagues. Medical professionals can do what they are trained to do without the burden of also having to run a business.

Kaiser fosters a sense of partnership between doctors and their patients. Caregiver and client explore health promotion and care options in an atmosphere of respect and friendliness. Patients can email their doctors with questions.

Kaiser also sponsors wellness programs, lectures, and client support groups to assist members in reaching their health goals. Members are regularly surveyed to get their response to the quality of care they have received.

Transitioning from Fee-for-Service to ACOs

The ACO movement has grown by leaps and bounds since passage of the ACA in 2010. By April 2015, 23.15 million additional patients were enrolled in ACOs, not counting those in Community Health Organizations. The percentage of physicians in solo or small group practice has diminished between 2000 and 2016 from 57% down to 33%. Indeed, ACOs are expected to become the primary health care delivery system during the next ten years.

BlueCross Blue Shield, the nation's largest health insurance company, is moving away from the fee-for-service model toward the ACO model. In a report released through its national trade association on July 9, 2014 they explained why: **"There is no choice but to move away from a system that rewards high cost over high quality and efficient treatment."**

The High Cost of Poverty

A small group of patients spend most of the money on health care in any given year. In 2010, 1% of patients spent 21% of the money and 14% spent 70% of the total. New research has revealed who these people are and why their care is so costly.

They are, for the most part, older, chronically ill, poor people that we as a society have cast aside, assuming that we were saving money by ignoring their needs. They have been without health insurance or regular medical care, living in highly stressful conditions, often for most of their lives.

Here are some common characteristics:

- Without a "medical home," they use the hospital emergency room for their many medical needs.

- They have several "advanced progressive chronic diseases," often including mental health problems.

- Whatever medical care they get is poorly coordinated.

- They have no home support to help with medications, proper food, or exercise.

- They often live in home conditions that lead to more medical problems—or they are homeless.

- They often do not have a telephone for follow up.

- Some do not speak English well and find it hard to communicate.

By changing our approach to treating this population, we have the potential to save $320 billion annually, according to Oliver Wyman, an international management consulting company that has studied this issue extensively and reported their findings in the *Health Care Blog*.

How do we manage their treatment in order to realize these savings?

A health care team is provided for each patient, including a medical doctor, a case manager, a home health aide, and a nutritionist. The patient is followed and treated by the same team whether in the hospital or at home. The whole person is considered, including housing and living conditions. The team strives to treat every patient with joy and dignity.

The Oliver Wyman research group has pinpointed the amount and categories of annual savings associated with this new treatment model:

- $150 billion from a 33% reduction of the amount of time spent in hospitals,

- $75 billion from a 27% reduction in outpatient care,

- $60 billion from a 30% reduction in care by specialists that is enabled by increased primary care, and

- $15 billion in smaller savings, primarily from reductions in pharmacy expenses.

The Oliver Wyman group is not just projecting its best estimates of savings in the abstract. It is basing them on examples of medical groups who are putting this model of care into practice with this population.

Two examples are (1) IORI Health, a private enterprise in Cambridge, Massachusetts that is profitable and growing with the help of hedge fund investors and (2) Care More, a company based in California and expanding. It serves seniors with many health problems with a focus on wellness. Their contract with Medicare pays a set amount per year.

An article in the *Journal of the American Medical Association,* January 2016, "Delivery Model for High Risk Older Patients: Back to the Future," confirms the success of these and other groups and writes of "the powerful potential in this model based on current best practices."

Hospitals are beginning to provide family doctors, visiting nurses, and home health aides. Accountable Care Organizations also provide these services in some areas. We are actively searching for better, less expensive ways to treat the legitimate health needs of those who have developed many chronic health problems. One percent of patients should not be spending 21% of health care dollars because of neglect and inefficiency in the system!

New Options for Long Term Care

Nursing home costs have increased by 4% annually for the past 10 years and now average $83,950 per year. Less intensive care in an assisted living facility now costs an average of $41,400 per year. Health care in one's own home usually costs much less, depending on the circumstances. Most elderly people prefer to stay in their own homes with medical visits and the assistance of home health aides, when their health status allows. The rational choice is to use the least intrusive, least expensive option and—only as a last ditch necessity--move to a nursing home.

Medicare pays only for short-term care in a nursing home while recovering from specific illnesses, not for long-term care. Medicaid—for those who have exhausted their personal savings—pays for care in a nursing home but not usually for intermediate care or home care. More than half of all Medicaid money is now spent on nursing homes. Why?

When the Social Security Act of 1933 was passed, professional nursing homes offered better care than any alternative. Hence Section 1915(c)—authorizing nursing home care as the standard for those who were too frail to live independently—was inserted to protect seniors from poor quality service. However, that same law says that, if it can be demonstrated that quality care can be obtained in another setting that is more desirable at a lower cost, the state can get a waiver that allows Medicaid payment for the better plan. Until the ACA there was precious little research that demonstrated the superior use of alternative methods of care. Now research and demonstration projects are flourishing and the system is evolving.

One such demonstration is the "Independence at Home Demonstration" that serves the frail elderly and/or the chronically ill population. The Demonstration has 14 sites in various parts of the country. A team agrees to serve a minimum of 200 patients in their homes. The care must be "comprehensive, continuous and accessible." The staff must be available for emergency care at any hour. Electronic records are kept on each service to each client. The group must purchase a van with a mobile diagnostic center. They agree to provide the total needs of their clients for a year at a single price. They then receive incentives for savings and good health outcomes. The demonstration includes a program to reduce wasteful dispensing of drugs, so common now in nursing homes.

Medicaid now spends more than half of its total outlay of funds on nursing home care. That total cost for FY 2014 was $492.3 billion or around $250 billion spent on nursing home care. If half that population can be served through home care models and half of that cost is saved—a reasonable assumption—some $60 billion dollars can be saved annually, while providing a more humane and personally satisfying quality of life for much of the elderly population.

Savings from Efficient and Humane End-of-Life Care

Finally, Medicare statistics show that 30% of total Medicare spending is for the 5% of beneficiaries who die each year. One-third of that cost comes in the last month of life. 2014 saw a total Medicare expenditure of $580 billion. The amount spent by 5% of Medicare recipients in the last year of life was $175 billion. How is that money typically spent? The patient is in a hospital, often in intensive care, undergoing invasive treatments that do little or nothing to prolong life, let alone improve the quality of the life that remains.

The Hospice program has emerged as a humane alternative to spending the final days or months of life in a hospital, kept alive by wires and tubes. The dying person is given the option to go home or to a hospice facility and spend this last phase of life with family and friends. Hospice care givers provide physical care and emotional support and make sure the person is not enduring unnecessary pain. Death comes with dignity. For many it is a welcome alternative to the medical model used in most hospitals.

The Affordable Care Act pays for one hour of a doctor's time to counsel with the dying person and family members, providing information about their options, considering their specific condition, as they decide whether to stay in the hospital or enter a hospice program. The decision is left to the patient and family, and the medical professionals follow their wishes.

When the hospice option becomes known and available across the country, as much as $50 billion annually may be saved from this $175 billion spent on the last month of life, beyond what is already saved by hospice programs.

Chapter 6

Managing Big Player Costs

Introduction

The big players get most of the money for our health care. Until the Affordable Care Act there was no serious effort to manage what these players charged for their services. All of them sought a non-competitive culture in which they controlled their charges and profits. It is no surprise then that these charges spiraled ever upward, always increasing the profit margins of the players. Let us see how the ACA has sought to protect the public against over-charging by each player.

A.   Physicians

Physician Pricing System Revised

How much should physicians be paid for each of the hundreds of procedures they perform? Who should decide? The traditional model gave the power to the American Medical Association, the chief lobbying group for the doctors. Cost to the patient or insurance company was based on the amount of time the procedure takes plus the skill-level involved. A *Washington Post* investigation found that the AMA committee regularly exaggerated the time a procedure takes. Following this revelation, Medicare officials assumed the power given them in the ACA to set rates for payment of physicians.

CMS now sets its own fee schedule based on independent study. The schedule covers 10,000 physicians who serve Medicare patients. Rates are being lowered gradually over four years to give physicians time to adjust. As the system transitions further from fee-for-service to ACOs, more physicians will be earning a good living on the salaries they are paid.

Some Physicians Abuse Their Profit Centers

Physicians often look for ways to invest some of the money they are making. A group of doctors pool their money and buy or build their own hospital to which they then send patients. Clearly there is opportunity for overuse and conflict of interest. And clearly, it happens.

More commonly, physicians set up their own labs or buy expensive diagnostic equipment to use in their offices with their own patients. Dr. Lawrence Maker, M.D. of

Stanford University studied the overuse of hospitals and office equipment when doctors own them. He found "unnecessary and unwanted care that was often harmful in 10% to 30% of treatment."   The President's budget in2016 called for eliminating this self-serving practice. The CBO estimated it would save $6.2 billion in 10 years. Virtually all Republicans oppose ending the practice.

Eliminating Unnecessary Medical Procedures

There are dozens of costly medical procedures that are often unnecessary. Here are two examples:

- Spinal Fusion Operations. More than 465,000 spinal fusion operations were performed in the United States in 2011, up from 56,000 in 1994. The total cost went from $47 million to $26 billion. Medical groups that have studied the issue are being generous when they state that at least half these procedures are unjustified. The public became aware of the issue when newspapers reported that a star surgeon in Daytona Beach, Florida, Dr. Federico Vinas, earned $1.9 million on average per year by performing spinal fusion operations. The hospital received $80,000 per operation. Under pressure from Medicare, the hospital agreed to have an independent group of outstanding doctors review these surgeries to determine if they were medically necessary. 10 random cases were chosen for review. The reviewing board concluded that 9 of the 10 surgeries were not medically necessary.

- CT Scans. Consumer Reports (CR) reviewed a study in the ***Journal of the American Medical Society*** which found that 80 million CT scans are done each year. They concluded that at least a third of these scans served no medical purpose and unnecessarily exposed patients to dangerous radiation. The overuse of the scan, the report found, will lead to the death of at least 2% of cancer patients, or 15,000 deaths per year. They concluded that 26,665,000 unnecessary scans were conducted at an average cost of $1,178 per scan.

B.   Insurance Companies

Capping Profits

Before the ACA, insurance companies could take as much profit as they could get from the market. On average, they took 26% of every dollar of a health insurance premium for overhead and profit.

The ACA limits overhead and profit to 15% for group policies and 20% for individual ones. Excess profits, by law, are returned to policy holders. In 2013, 8.5 million

Americans got rebates from their health insurance providers. They had been overcharged. The total rebate amounted to over $500 million.

Critics say the law is weak in that it leaves the task of enforcement to the states. Only states have the authority to regulate the insurance companies operating in their state. The ACA provides money for each state to review the financial records of its insurance companies to determine if rate increases are justified. Some states give their regulators legal authority to veto rates deemed excessive. Other states can review rate increases in advance and publish their findings that rates are excessive but lack the legal power to veto them. Other states give their insurers a free hand to set rates. State governments with regulators in the pocket of the insurance industry can still do great harm to their citizens.

A 2012 report by HHS stated that state regulators challenging insurance industry rate hikes had saved their citizens $1.2 billion on their insurance premiums.

Marketplace Competition is Lowering Costs

HHS released a report on June 18, 2014 about how the new federal exchanges were affecting marketplace competition and prices in the 36 states using the exchanges. Prior to the ACA, there was little competition among insurance companies. Indeed, a single player had the entire market in 30 states and the District of Columbia. The 2014 study found:

- Four out of five enrollees live in states with at least three insurance companies competing for their business.

- Cost to purchasers went down by 4% for each additional company entering the marketplace.

- Overall growth in the cost of the Silver Plan in the 35 states with federal exchanges increased by only 2% on average in 2015 over the prior year.

- There were 25% more issuers in the marketplace in 2015 than in 2014.

- Premiums in counties with three or more insurers cost 9% less than in counties with one or two providers.

Federal exchanges are working as intended. They increase competition and hence lower the cost to policy holders. However, rates depend on oversight by state insurance commissions—still lacking or hobbled by anti-regulatory politics in too many states.

C.   Hospitals

Revising Hospital Costs

We spend $700 billion per year for our hospital care. Prior to the ACA very little thought was given to how well we were spending our hospital money. The whole enterprise grew topsy-turvy with virtually no oversight.

The ACA noted that most hospitals were inefficient—and often dangerous, with unacceptable levels of medical errors and hospital-acquired infections. The ACA challenges hospitals to clean up and lower costs. To track progress, it now requires transparency for all hospital records. The Act established a "Medical Reimbursement Data Center" in every region. One of its purposes is to "develop fee schedules and other data-based rates…." These Data Centers also monitor medical procedures and outcomes to determine if hospitals are providing good care at a lower cost.

The ACA authorized two specific programs that reduce costs and save lives—the Hospital Readmission Reduction Program and the Hospital Acquired Conditions Reduction Program.

Hospital Readmission Reduction Program

This program began in October 2012 with the goal of lowering excess readmission rates within 30 days after leaving the hospital. These readmissions are amazingly common and costly. Nearly one in five Medicaid patients, for example, returns to a hospital within a month of discharge. A CMS study showed that nearly three-quarters of readmissions are preventable.

What are the problems and how are they addressed? Some patients are sent home with new illnesses contracted while in the hospital. Others were treated for the wrong diagnosis. Some are released before they are able to care for themselves without any consideration of whether they have anyone to help them at home. Others cannot understand the written directions prepared for their care. Some fail to get or take their medications. Without appropriate support these people are back in the hospital within a month. Relatively inexpensive procedures and follow-up with home visits by nurses and health aides can dramatically lower cost by keeping this population from having to return to the hospital unnecessarily.

Hospital Acquired Conditions Reduction Program

Dr. Chauncey Crandell warned in his **Heart Health Report**, "No matter how brief your stay in the hospital, the moment you exchange your clothes for a hospital gown, you are putting your health in peril…. In the United States about 100,000 persons die each year from infections they acquire in a hospital."

The first order of business for the Hospital Acquired Conditions Reduction Program was to conduct a study in every hospital in the country to investigate the rate of infections and the estimated cost, along with the number of preventable deaths. The findings for each hospital are now posted online. Next, the program instituted best-practice prevention procedures for hospital staff and financial incentives for hospitals to lower their infection rates. The efforts to clean up the hospitals had the following results between 2011 and 2013:

- A 17% decline or 1.3 million fewer acquired illnesses among discharged patients,

- 50,000 fewer hospital patients died, thanks to this ACA program, and

- $12 billion in health costs were saved in three years because these safety measures were in effect.

Murky Hospital Billing

Before the ACA, patients had no way to know if hospital charges were fair. In fact, hospitals had successfully lobbied states to require them to keep charges hidden.

Medicare now reviews hospital charges, and the previously clueless, vulnerable public now has access to all hospital charges online. For example, joint replacements cost Medicare $52,063 on average in 2012. At the low end was Ada, Oklahoma, where Medicare was charged $5,304. At the high end was Monterey, California, where the same procedure cost Medicare $427,207. Medicare now challenges rates such as those in Monterey that are clearly out of line.

Further, in the traditional payment model hospitals "code in" each service provided to a patient. The patient has no way to know what the codes mean or whether charges are accurate. Mistakes are made in entering the code, so that a unit of 0.2 can become 2.0, increasing the cost from $200 to $2,000. Note how hospital bills are affected by the lowly intravenous bag of salt water. An IV bag holds just over a quart of water with less than two teaspoons of salt. Over a billion units a year are sold in hospitals. The average cost to the hospital was 46 cents in 2010, rising to $1.07 in 2013. How are IV bags billed to patients? Data show the cost varied greatly. Some patient bills are 200 to 300 times the actual cost. Some are coded "IV therapy" at 1,000 times the cost. Others coded "IV administration" have a different price.

As a practical matter, the patient has no way to determine the fairness of charges, and indeed, insurance companies and government struggle with the same problem. Now, with increased billing transparency, they at least have a better handle on how to evaluate and challenge the hospitals.

The new system is moving toward paying a pre-set fee for an operation or medical procedure rather than a hodge-podge of "fees" for each element of the "services" rendered.

The Hospital's Secret Books

The new transparency reveals what was long suspected—hospitals keep two sets of books. One is the charge that is advertised. The other is the amount they actually get paid. Hospitals negotiate better prices with all their major clients—including insurance companies, self-insuring corporations and ACOs—and give the best prices to those who bring them the most business. An individual without insurance will often pay double the amount an insurance company pays for the identical service—another argument in favor of health insurance for everyone.

Hospitals are Being Transformed

An arm of the American Hospital Association held its annual meeting in Chicago on September 20-22, 2015. The title for the conference reflected the challenges and opportunities facing America's hospitals: "The New Landscape for Health Care Deliverance: Consumer-centric, Outcomes-focused, Value-driven."

Hospitals are now evaluated both by the ACA and by patient surveys. Now Medicare and most insurance companies will no longer pay for the mistakes made by hospital staff. Now charges are checked and potential overcharges are investigated. Hospitals that rise to the challenge of focusing on patients, improving outcomes and lowering costs are recognized and rewarded. Those that don't are also recognized—and penalized.

The Virginia Hospital Center in Arlington is an award-winning example. It has the distinction of being "one of the 100 best hospitals in the country" and "one of the 50 best cardiovascular hospitals in America." A study found that among the 50 best heart disease hospitals, the winning hospitals spent $2,700 less per by-pass surgery and $1,700 less per admitted heart-attack patient. Patients who undergo coronary bypass surgery at VHC have 40% fewer readmissions, 60% fewer deaths, and 75% fewer reoperations than at the average hospital in the country. More than 80% of patients give the hospital a high rating of 9 or 10 on surveys. And note that VHA had the lowest average cost per patient in Northern Virginia at $6,022. A companion hospital, Fairfax Inova, in Fairfax County had a cost per patient in 2013 of $9,384—35% higher.

The lesson from this example is that as quality goes up, the cost of care can go down. This remarkable fact is being demonstrated across the country and throughout the hospital system.

D.   Durable Medical Equipment

Medicare paid far too much for durable medical equipment before the ACA—simply paying whatever suppliers charged without question. Of course, the senior citizen paid 20% of the cost.

The ACA gave authority to Medicare to design new rate schedules. On January 1, 2011 Medicare introduced competitive bidding as an experiment in nine areas of the country with a limited number of items. In its first year this experiment saved 42% in the areas where it was tried. Round two began July 1, 2013 and expanded into 91 additional areas with a much larger number of items covered. Medicare spends about $7 billion per year on durable medical equipment and expects to save 40% or $2.8 billion when this new model is fully operational, a projected $29 billion in 10 years.

E.   Pharmaceuticals

The pharmaceutical industry represents 9.3% of the nation's health care expenditures. We spend about $300 billion per year at the pharmacy. Drug costs are difficult to control and are still rising rapidly because the makers have lobbied successfully for special privileges. At every possible turn the ACA is challenging excessive drug costs.

The ACA recognizes that billions of dollars can be saved by using more generics, the less expensive equivalent of original expensive versions. A study conducted by *Consumer Reports* found that during doctor visits, patients were only told 5% of the time when they could use a generic rather than a prescription drug. That is changing. A 2013 report found that in 2012 generics saved the U.S. health system $217 billion, up from $188 billion in 2011.

Overpricing Breakout Drugs

The question facing our society is how to treat pricing when only a single effective drug is available or when a break-through drug is new on the market. An example illustrates the dilemma: Sovaldi is a recently developed drug that when used with a companion drug is the first successful treatment for hepatitis C (HCV). Gilead Science bought Sovaldi and charges $2,000 per day for 90 days to take the entire regimen and become free of the deadly disease. With all of the profit on each pill, John C. Martin, CEO of Gilead has stock now worth $1.2 billion.

Gilead Science is functioning lawfully. A Republican Congress passed a law in 2006 forbidding Medicare from negotiating with drug companies for lower prices. With their patent, Gilead can charge any outrageous amount it chooses.

Should society "grin and bear it" and pay up, as we are doing now? Michael Weinstein, President of the AIDS Healthcare Foundation in Los Angeles, said of the cost of Sovaldi, "It is the poster child for everything that is wrong with drug prices." There is a growing consensus that society simply cannot afford to keep making these exorbitant ransom payments for its citizens' lives. This is unfinished business for the ACA that will not go away. It has recently become an issue in the Democratic Presidential campaign.

Cost of Cancer Drug Development

Two distinguished Professors of Medicine, one of whom is a Professor of Medical Ethics at Harvard Medical School, challenged drug companies who claim it costs $1.3 billion to bring a new cancer drug to market. The makers say they are justified in charging more than $100,000 per patient because of this huge upfront cost. The professors analyze this $1.3 billion claim:

- Half of that estimate is not research cost, but rather a high "opportunity cost" figure for profits that drug companies could have made by investing the research money in stocks and bonds. Eliminating this projection brings the actual research costs down to $650 million.

- Taxpayers subsidize about half of company research costs through credits on their corporate taxes. This brings the real cost down to $325 million.

- Industry's $1.3 billion cost is based on a sample of the most expensive fifth of new drugs, not the average of all drugs. Correcting this distortion brings the cost down to $230 million.

- A few expensive projects always inflate the overall average so it is more accurate to use the median cost—the point where half of the projects costs more and half less. This lowers company research costs to $170 billion.

- Finally, companies build on research that is actually carried out by the National Institutes of Health and the National Cancer Institute, bringing their own actual cost down to the median of $125 million.

These conclusions bring the professors to ask, "Why are cancer drugs so expensive?" They also note that new drugs with more inflated prices are often no better or only slightly better than older ones. Finally, they note that prices on their older drugs have almost doubled over the past ten years, with no new cost to the companies.

The conclusion by these distinguished professors is that Congress needs to challenge the drug companies on their pricing. They note that no other country allows companies to raise prices on their older drugs. Neither can they set prices without regard to the common good. "And it should eliminate the rule that prohibits Medicare from negotiating discount drug prices. The changes would substantially cut the nation's health care cost."

Chapter 7

Savings through Preventive Care

Finding Savings from Staying Healthy

We expect to save billions more through preventive medical services such as cancer screening, cholesterol management, vaccines and birth control. The ACA emphasizes wellness and saves money for the health care system through public awareness campaigns and incentive programs for stopping smoking, reducing obesity, improving nutrition and encouraging exercise.

Smoking Cessation

The Affordable Care Act funds programs to help people stop smoking. Public awareness programs began all the way back in 1950 when more than half the country smoked and 400,000 persons died each year from lung cancer. Through public awareness programs and legal action against tobacco companies, the percentage of smokers had dropped to 20% by the time the ACA was enacted. Through new ACA initiatives it dropped to 17.8% in 2015.

A new California Medical Association study uncovered the staggering public cost of the tobacco habit. "In California the cost of a single smoker throughout life is $1.5 million, including more than $182,000 in healthcare costs. The total cost is nearly $30,000 per year, including over $3,500 in health costs each year the person smokes."

From this experience with tobacco the authors of the ACA learned that public awareness programs can change behavior and improve health outcomes. In the process they save a lot of money.

Dealing with Obesity

The United States is in the midst of an obesity crisis. Over half the population is overweight and 25% are obese. The human and financial costs are staggering. The Robert Wood Johnson Foundation estimates the cost of preventable diabetes caused by obesity ranges from $147 billion annually to $210 billion per year. Health care costs are 52% higher than for persons whose weight falls in the normal range. Medicare costs are $1,723 more each year for the obese senior.

There is strong evidence that we can address obesity in much the same way we addressed smoking. The ACA has many tools in its kit: It requires fast food restaurants and chains to post calorie content of their food. It is emphasizing healthy eating in public schools. Workers are getting exercise facilities in places of employment with tax breaks for owners. Employees also get a reduction in their health insurance rates by being part of a weight loss program. Medical school curriculums are now emphasizing the importance of keeping an eye on weight control and how to achieve it. Nutritional labeling is now required on all packaged foods.

Chapter 8

Moving forward with the ACA — Challenges and Opportunities

Republican Replacement Plans

Republicans in the U. S. House of Representatives voted to "Repeal and Replace" the Affordable Care Act more than 60 times. Each of the 14 Republican primary candidates for President vowed to "repeal and replace" when they took over leadership of the country. While "repeal" has been pushed relentlessly and loudly, the plans to "replace" have been paltry and poorly publicized.

Nevertheless, some replacement plans have surfaced, including several by Republican candidates for President and the plan put forth in April 2016 by the House Republican Study Committee.

They are all similar, with a few unique features in each.

Republican plans are built around Health Savings Accounts in which individuals set aside $5,000 to $7,000 annually tax free and then draw out of this account to pay their medical bills. When persons have as much as $200,000 in savings they can afford a low cost health insurance plan that pays only 50% of large medical expenses. They also receive some tax credits.

The plan works well for the upper middle class and the wealthy, but for the majority of hourly income people with virtually no savings it is impossible to find the money for that level of saving. And it would take many years to build up the reserves to justify a catastrophic health insurance policy, which is also projected.

Further, the Republican plans eliminate employer-sponsored health care insurance. But most employees do not make enough to put aside $5,000 each year in savings or benefit from the tax credits that are to replace employer plans, in place for the past 70 years. Eliminating employer-sponsored insurance without a safer option would simply throw millions more people out of insurance. **These plans makes the rich richer (new tax breaks, lower business expenses) and the poor poorer (higher priced insurance without the income to buy it).**

Under the Republican plans the average family would pay 25% of their income for medical expenses—a sheer impossibility for most families.

The bottom line: these plans offer short-sighted saving for the government by leaving 28 million Americans to face sickness and death without proper health care. Again, the population is at the mercy of the old "pay or die" system. By taking the most generous features from these Republican plans they might make it possible for 3 million people to get insurance--while cutting 25 million from the rolls. At the same time we lose all of the cost-saving benefits of the ACA—the $100 billion in savings to Uncle Sam each year, the $2,600 lower insurance policy for the average family, and the $1,000 lower actual cost of Medicare for every senior in the nation.

It gets worse. Under these Republican plans the federal government caps the amount it sends back to states to pay for Medicaid and other social and welfare programs. The amount is set at a much lower level than the combined cost of these programs now. Each state would then decide how to spend the money. They could even use it to lower taxes for the rich!

The repeal of the Affordable Care Act ends the financial protection for persons with preexisting conditions. Gone are all of the preventive measures that save money by focusing on building health rather than treating sickness. Gone are the measures to upgrade and hold accountable the hospitals of the nation. Gone are the efforts to control costs by limiting unwarranted profits of doctors, insurance companies, hospitals, medical device markers and drug companies. No program remains to help the country move from an inefficient, overused "fee for service" model to a lower cost, higher quality Accountable Care Organization model.

A Republican President would wipe out countless benefits of the ACA with the stroke of a pen his "first day in office." Hence, our first order of business is to prevent a Republican from getting to the White House.

Opportunities for Progress

The Affordable Care Act is not perfect. However, it is far better than most people realize, in the light of relentless Republican disinformation—and a lack of consistent, full-throated support from Democrats. It is the only health care reform bill that could have been passed at the time, and it was passed at great cost in political capital, without a single Republican vote in either house of Congress, and even without a few Democratic votes.

Through the ACA, our nation has begun the immense task of bringing coherence and inclusiveness to our health care system. The ACA did not eliminate private enterprise and profit from the system, but it did restrain runaway profits in crucial sectors of the system and introduce the tools and transparencies to make further improvements possible.

Much waste and profiteering remains to be eliminated from the system, particularly in the pharmaceutical sector. Companies motivated primarily by profit will try to co-opt progress from the public interest. Continued progress will require public engagement, vigilance, and demand for good governance. It will require the election of a President who believes in and supports the ACA.

With the ACA in place as a foundation and with the private sector having time to adapt to change, it may be feasible to incorporate a "public option," perhaps allowing citizens under 65 to buy into Medicare, with a gradual lowering of the age of eligibility.

The Importance of Electing Down-Ticket Democrats

To maximize the ACA's potential for good, it is vital to liberate states from Republican control. We have seen the devastation wrought for lower income Americans by the Supreme Court decision to allow states to opt out of the Medicaid expansion portion of the ACA. This has left millions of poor and lower income Americans without coverage and damaged the economies of the Republican-controlled states that refused these Federal subsidies on behalf of their citizens. **Voters need to rise up and demand to be included.**

Similarly, the insurance industry still operates state by state. Each state has an Insurance Commission or similar regulatory body responsible for overseeing the insurance companies that operate in their state. Although the ACA provides support to the states to beef up their regulatory capabilities, many Republican-controlled state governments with an anti-regulatory ideology continue to neglect this oversight function. In the pockets of the big insurance companies, they do not work on behalf of their citizens to scrutinize proposed rate hikes and prevent those that are not justified. Insurance rates have risen unnecessarily in many Republican-controlled states, especially rural states that also lack robust competition among insurance companies.

For the full potential of the Affordable Care Act to be realized and built upon, we must also take back Congress and the state governments on behalf of Democrats working for the public good.

About the Author

Robert L McCan has devoted his life to social justice. His first career was as a Yale Divinity School-educated Southern Baptist minister, deeply rooted in the Christian tradition that recognizes the "social gospel" as coequal with the gospel of personal salvation. He earned his Ph.D. in Ethics and Church History at the University of Edinburgh, Scotland.

After being forced to resign by his Virginia congregation over his support for the Civil Rights movement, Dr. McCan left the pastoral ministry and became a Visiting Scholar with Faculty Status at Harvard University, where he prepared for creating an international college with faculty and students from all parts of the world, where participants learned to live together in a global community. Dr. McCan pioneered what later became the multi-cultural approach to education as the founder of Dag Hammarskjold College.

During the remainder of his professional career, he alternated between government service and higher education. He held Executive Appointments in four federal agencies, all with public policy components: the U.S. Office of Economic Opportunity, the U.S. Office of Education, the Agency for International Development and the Woodrow Wilson International Center for Scholars, where as Deputy to the Director he dealt daily with public policy at the highest level.

After his years of government service, Dr. McCan became Associate Professor of Political Ethics at Wesley Theological Seminary, American University. There he directed the "Washington Semester for Seminarians" program, in which theology students studied and participated first-hand the political process from an ethical perspective. He was also employed by The Churches' Center for Theology and Public Policy, a think-tank supported by Protestant denominations and Catholic Bishops to provide guidance for them on public policy issues. Finally, he was a long-time leader and served for four years as President of the United Nations Association for the National Capitol Area.

Bob McCan lives with his wife Peggy in Falls Church Virginia. He is active in the Episcopal Church and in the political process. His recent books include *Justice for Gays and Lesbians* and the two editions of *Citizen's Guide to Health Care Reform*.